SUPER CROC

Paul Sereno's Dinosaur Eater

by Paul Sereno
and Natalie Lunis

BEARPORT
PUBLISHING

New York, New York

Credits

Cover, © Reuters / Corbis; Title Page, © Mike Hettwer / Project Exploration; 4, © Mike Hettwer / Project Exploration; 5, © Mike Hettwer / Project Exploration; 7, © John Sibbick; 8, © Mike Hettwer / Project Exploration; 9, © Mike Hettwer / Project Exploration; 10, © Christian Montenat; 11, © Philippe Taquet; 12, © Paul C. Sereno / Project Exploration; 13, © Mike Hettwer / Project Exploration; 14, © Mike Hettwer / Project Exploration; 15, © AP Wide World Photos; 16, © Zigmund Leszczynski / Animals Animals – Earth Scenes; 17T, © Gavriel Jecan / Corbis; 17B, © Zigmund Leszczynski / Animals Animals – Earth Scenes; 18, © Royalty-Free/Corbis; 19, © Mike Hettwer / Project Exploration; 20, © Robert Clark; 21, © Shutterstock; 22, © Mike Hettwer / Project Exploration; 23, © Claus Meyer / Minden Pictures; 24, © Gary Staab Studio; 25T, © Gary Staab Studio; 25B, © Gary Staab Studio; 26, © AP Wide World Photos; 27, © Reuters / Corbis; 28–29 Rodica Prato; 28, Kathrin Ayer; 29T, © Dorling Kindersley Media Library; 29B, Kathrin Ayer.

Publisher: Kenn Goin
Editorial Director: Adam Siegel
Creative Director: Spencer Brinker
Photo Researcher: Beaura Kathy Ringrose
Design: Dawn Beard Creative

Library of Congress Cataloging-in-Publication Data
Sereno, Paul C.
  Supercroc : Paul Sereno's dinosaur eater / by Paul Sereno and Natalie Lunis.
     p. cm. — (Fossil hunters)
  Includes bibliographical references and index.
  ISBN-13: 978-1-59716-255-5 (library binding)
  ISBN-10: 1-59716-255-8 (library binding)
  ISBN-13: 978-1-59716-283-8 (pbk.)
  ISBN-10: 1-59716-283-3 (pbk.)
  1. Crocodiles, Fossil—Juvenile literature. 2. Dinosaurs—Juvenile literature. I. Lunis, Natalie. II. Title. III. Series.

  QE862.C8S47 2007
  567.9'8—dc22

                              2006013796

For more information, write to Bearport Publishing Company, Inc., 101 Fifth Avenue, Suite 6R, New York, New York 10003. Printed in the United States of America.

10 9 8 7 6 5 4 3 2 1

Table of Contents

Skull in the Sand

The huge skull poked out of the hot sand. Paul Sereno and his team brushed some of the sand away. They then chipped at the rock that clung to the creature's bones. Finally, they could see the whole skull.

The skull's lower jaw alone was nearly six feet (1.8 m) long.

Paul lay down and stretched out on the ground next to the giant **fossil**. They were both the same size—about six feet (1.8 m) long.

After Paul got up, the whole team looked on in awe. They had uncovered the skull of a gigantic crocodile—in the middle of the world's largest desert.

Paul brushes away sand from the huge crocodile's bones.

Crocodile skulls are stronger than the skulls of almost any other **prehistoric** animal. As a result, they are more likely to survive as fossils.

Killer in the Water

Paul Sereno is a **paleontologist**. He had come to the country of Niger (nee-ZHAIR) to search part of Africa's vast Sahara Desert. His plan was to look for dinosaur bones. Yet Paul was not shocked to find the huge skull of an **extinct** crocodile.

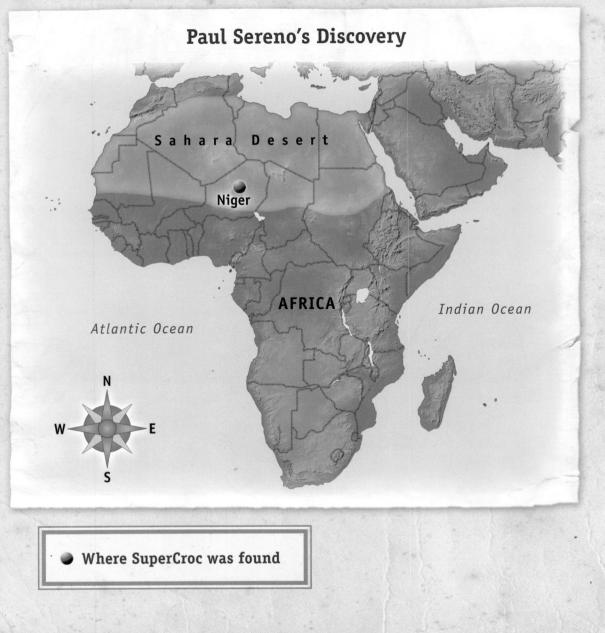

Paul Sereno's Discovery

Sahara Desert

Niger

AFRICA

Atlantic Ocean

Indian Ocean

N
W   E
S

● Where SuperCroc was found

Paul knew that the Sahara was once very different. Millions of years ago, wide rivers flowed there. Fish, turtles, and crocodiles swam in the waters. Dinosaurs came to the riverbanks to drink. Some of them never left. For Paul, the gigantic crocodile skull told the story. This crocodile ate dinosaurs.

A plant-eating dinosaur called *Ouranosaurus* (oo-*ran*-oh-SOR-uhss) was probably one of the animals that the giant crocodile ate.

This illustration shows what *Ouranosaurus* might have looked like.

Finding More Fossils

"We had never seen anything like it," Paul explained. "The snout and teeth were designed for grabbing **prey**—fish, turtles, and dinosaurs that strayed too close."

Fortunately, the team found more than just the gigantic skull. During **expeditions** in 1997 and 2000, they dug up bones from the crocodile's back and legs. They also unearthed many bony plates called **scutes**.

Scutes form **armor** that protects a crocodile's neck, back, and tail.

This is a scute from the crocodile Paul found. The largest scute was almost one foot (.3 m) long.

Fossils from other kinds of crocodiles turned up as well. These crocodiles were not as large as the one with the nearly six-foot (1.8 m) skull, however. That croc "was the monster of them all," according to Paul.

The team's finds included more skulls from the same kind of giant crocodile. This spot contained two skulls side by side, one an adult and the other a young crocodile half its size.

The Flesh Crocodile Emperor

   Paul and his team were not the first people to discover fossils of this giant crocodile. In the 1940s, teeth, bones, and scutes from an unknown kind of crocodile were found in the Sahara. A few years later, in the 1950s, a **partial** skull was discovered.

   Then in 1965, French paleontologists traveled to the Sahara to collect the partial skull. The following year they named this **ancient** animal *Sarcosuchus imperator* (*sar*-koh-SOO-kuss im-PEER-ay-*tor*). The name means "flesh crocodile **emperor**."

In the 1940s, Albert-Félix de Lapparent was the first known person to discover fossils of the extinct crocodile.

Paul's team had discovered the first complete skull and many parts of this creature's skeleton. They also came up with its nickname—SuperCroc.

This is the giant crocodile skull that the French paleontologists studied.

New Pieces to an Old Puzzle

The French scientists had written about *Sarcosuchus*. Yet they were unable to answer many questions about this animal. After all, they had only had a few fossils to study. These fossils were the first pieces of a giant jigsaw puzzle.

A complete skull of *Sarcosuchus* is made up of about 60 separate bones. A complete skeleton is made up of about 250 bones.

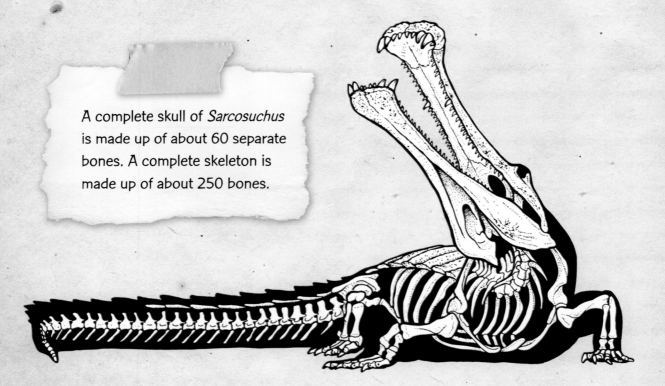

Paul was able to make this drawing of SuperCroc's skeleton based on the bones he found.

Paul's discovery added many more pieces. By the end of his second expedition in 2000, his team had found bones from several individual crocodiles. If these were put together, they could form half a skeleton of *Sarcosuchus*. They could also reveal many new facts about the emperor that had once ruled the river.

Paul's team lies down behind the giant lower jaws to imagine how big SuperCroc might have been.

The Search Goes On

Paul and his team packed up the bones and loaded them onto trucks. First the bones traveled across the desert. Then they traveled across an ocean. Finally, SuperCroc's bones arrived at the University of Chicago. For the next year, Paul and his students cleaned and studied the bones in his lab.

A preparator cleaning SuperCroc's bones

Experts who clean fossils are called preparators. Preparators sometimes use the same tools as dentists.

Paul learned where each bone belonged in the crocodile's skeleton. He also learned which bones were missing.

Paul's search for the bones had ended. Now he set out to discover how SuperCroc really looked and lived.

Paul talking about the discovery of SuperCroc

The Croc Family Tree

SuperCroc lived about 110 million years ago, during a time that scientists call the **Cretaceous period**. Many kinds of dinosaurs lived during this time, and so did many kinds of crocodiles.

Today, there are three main groups of living crocs—true crocodiles, alligators, and gharials. They all live in regions of the world that are wet and warm year-round. Together, these animals are known as **crocodilians**. There are 23 different **species** of crocodilians.

Crocodilians look similar in many ways. The main differences among the 23 species can be found in the size and shape of their snouts, as seen in these pictures.

Gharial

From its bones, Paul could tell that SuperCroc was not directly related to today's crocs. Other ancient crocodiles were their **ancestors**. Still, SuperCroc was similar in many ways to today's crocodiles. These modern crocs could offer many clues about the way SuperCroc looked and lived.

Saltwater crocodile

Crocodiles and dinosaurs are both **descendants** of ancient reptiles called archosaurs.

American alligator

Hiding and Hunting

Modern crocodiles are fierce hunters. With only their eyes and **nostrils** poking out of the water, crocs can float almost invisibly. They wait silently for a victim to get close enough. Then they attack, snapping their jaws shut in a flash.

Like this modern crocodile, SuperCroc probably spent much of its time hiding in the water.

A crocodile usually pulls its prey into the water, drowning it before tearing it apart.

Next they tear off pieces of their prey and swallow them whole. Crocodiles eat this way because their sharp teeth are shaped for grabbing and biting through flesh—not for chewing.

After studying SuperCroc's skull and teeth, Paul concluded that the ancient croc must have hunted in the same way. Silently cruising the ancient river, it lived an "**ambush** lifestyle," he thinks.

Paul learned that SuperCroc had more than 130 teeth—all extremely strong and shaped for grabbing prey.

A Big Bite

Among today's **predators**, crocodilians have the most powerful bite. How can scientists be sure? They use a tool called a bite bar. It measures an animal's **bite force**.

Working with crocodile experts, Paul set out to find SuperCroc's bite force. The scientists encouraged different crocs and gators to chomp down on the bite bar. They recorded each animal's size and its bite force.

A scientist gets ready to measure an alligator's bite force.

From their **data**, they concluded that SuperCroc had a bite force of 18,000 pounds (8,165 kg). How strong is that? As one researcher explained, being trapped in SuperCroc's jaws would feel like being caught under the tire of a Mack truck.

Scientists think that SuperCroc might have had an even more powerful bite than *T. rex*.

The largest living crocodile today has a bite force of about 2,125 pounds (964 kg).

Measuring Up

Paul and other scientists used information about crocodiles alive today to **estimate** SuperCroc's bite force. They measured and tested crocodiles of different sizes. They could tell that the bigger the crocodile, the bigger the bite force.

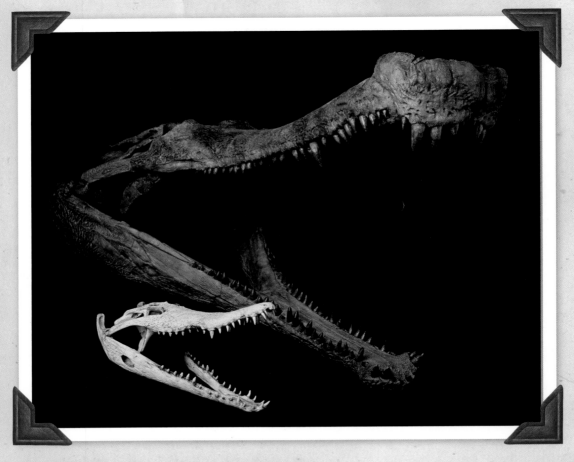

This photo shows how large SuperCroc's skull is compared to today's Orinoco crocodile from South America.

SuperCroc was twice as big as the largest crocodile living today.

Paul figured he could also use today's crocodiles to estimate SuperCroc's total body length. He had an adult skull and half the bones of its body. Now he needed measurements for the largest living crocodile. So he traveled to Costa Rica and captured the biggest ones he could find. They were about 14 feet (4 m) long. Using these measurements, he concluded that SuperCroc was 40 feet (12 m) long. It was about the size of a city bus!

This is an American crocodile—the kind of crocodile that Paul measured in Costa Rica.

A Life-Size Model

No one knows exactly what *Sarcosuchus* looked like when it was alive. All Paul had was a fossil skull and bones from the skeleton. Still, he was determined to bring the 40-foot-long (12-m) reptile to life. To do so, he would need to team up with a special kind of artist.

Making SuperCroc's body

Paul sent artist Gary Staab sketches and casts of SuperCroc's skull and other bones. Gary would use them to make a life-size model of the world's largest crocodile. He needed supplies by the ton—including 5,000 pounds (2,268 kg) of clay, 80 gallons (303 l) of rubber, and 40,000 staples.

In four months, the job was done. SuperCroc, posed with jaws ready for action, seemed to come alive.

Adding SuperCroc's head to the model

The model is almost finished.

The real SuperCroc weighed an estimated 17,500 pounds (7,938 kg).

A Journey Across Time

SuperCroc now travels all over the world. It is the star of an **exhibit** called "The Science of SuperCroc." The ancient crocodile has made stops in Australia, Asia, Europe, South America, and many U.S. cities.

Visitors to the show can see the huge skull that Paul Sereno dug up. A few steps away is Gary Staab's giant, life-like model.

Paul with SuperCroc

Side by side, the two objects remind people about the creature's amazing journey. Once SuperCroc ruled a river as wide as the Mississippi, dining on dinosaurs. Then it lay buried in a desert. Today, it has reappeared to teach people about life on Earth millions of years ago.

The life-size model shows visitors what SuperCroc would have looked like in the flesh.

Sarcosuchus imperator died out about 100 million years ago—about 35 million years before the dinosaurs became extinct.

A Trip Back in Time: Who Lived with SuperCroc?

Dinosaurs roamed the earth for around 150 million years. Scientists divide the time in which the dinosaurs lived into three periods—the Triassic period (250 to 205 million years ago), the Jurassic period (205 to 145 million years ago), and the Cretaceous period (145 to 65 million years ago).

SuperCroc lived alongside dinosaurs during the middle of the Cretaceous period. Here are three dinosaurs that shared SuperCroc's world.

Ouranosaurus

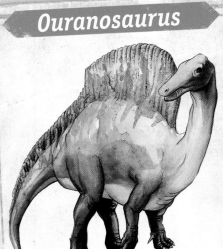

This plant-eater walked along Africa's riverbanks 110 million years ago. If it came too close to the water, it might have become SuperCroc's next meal.

FACTS

Ouranosaurus
(oo-ran-oh-SOR-uhss)

- has a name that means "brave lizard"
- had tall spines on its back that formed a sail
- used the sail, which may have been brightly colored, for displaying to others of its species
- could move on two legs or four
- **size:** 30–35 feet (9–11 m) long

Suchomimus

This fierce meat-eating dinosaur often went after the 5-foot-long (1.5-m) fish that shared the river with SuperCroc. As a result, it probably got into fierce fights with the giant crocodile.

FACTS

Suchomimus
(*sook*-oh-MYE-muhss)

- has a name that means "crocodile mimic"
- had crocodile-like jaws and one-foot-long (.3 m) claws that helped it catch fish
- like *Ouranosaurus*, had a sail along its back for display
- **size:** 36 feet (11 m) long

Nigersaurus

Drinking water along the riverbanks, this dinosaur would have had to keep an eye out for its main enemies—*Suchomimus* and SuperCroc.

FACTS

Nigersaurus
(*nee*-zhair-SOR-uhss)

- named after the country in Africa where it was found, Niger
- ate plants and had a long neck
- had as many as 1,000 small teeth in its jaws
- walked on all fours
- was a distant cousin of *Diplodocus*
- **size:** 45–50 feet (14–15 m) long

Glossary

ambush (AM-bush)
hiding and then suddenly attacking

ancestors (AN-sess-turz)
family members who lived a long time ago

ancient (AYN-shunt)
very old

armor (AR-mur)
a protective covering

bite force (BITE FORSS)
the power of an animal's bite

Cretaceous period
(kri-TAY-shuhss PIHR-ee-uhd)
a time period from about 145 to 65 million years ago, at the end of which dinosaurs became extinct

crocodilians (*krok*-uh-DIL-yuhnz)
a group of animals made up of crocodiles and their close relatives

data (DAY-tuh)
information often in the form of numbers

descendants (di-SEND-uhnts)
people or animals that come from a family that lived earlier in time

emperor (EM-pur-ur)
a ruler

estimate (ESS-ti-mate)
to make a careful guess about the size, cost, or value of something

exhibit (eg-ZIB-it)
something that is shown to many people

expeditions (*ek*-spuh-DISH-uhnz)
long trips taken for a specific reason, such as exploring

extinct (ek-STINGKT)
a kind of plant or animal that has died out; there are no more alive on Earth

fossil (FOSS-uhl)
the remains (often as petrified wood, shell, or bones) of plants or animals that lived long ago

nostrils (NOSS-truhlz)
openings in the nose that are used for breathing and smelling

paleontologist
(*pale*-ee-uhn-TOL-uh-jist)
a scientist who learns about ancient life by studying fossils

partial (PAR-shuhl)
not complete

predators (PRED-uh-turz)
animals that hunt other animals for food

prehistoric (*pree*-hi-STOR-ik)
more than 5,500 years ago, which was before the time when people began to use writing to record history

prey (PRAY)
animals that are hunted or caught for food

scutes (SKYOOTS)
bony plates that in crocodiles protect the neck, back, and tail

species (SPEE-sheez)
naturally occurring populations of living organisms that can reproduce

Bibliography

Sereno, Paul, Hans Larsson, Christian Sidor, and Boubé Gado. "The Giant Crocodyliform *Sarcosuchus* from the Cretaceous of Africa." *Science* 294 (November 2001): 1516–1519. Published online on October 25, 2001, at **www.sciencemag.org/cgi/content/abstract/294/5546/1516**.

Sloan, Christopher. *SuperCroc and the Origin of Crocodiles*. Washington, D.C.: National Geographic Society (2002).

SuperCroc (DVD). A National Geographic Channel Presentation (2002).

Taquet, Philippe. *Dinosaur Impressions: Postcards from a Paleontologist*. New York: Cambridge University Press (1998).

Read More

Cohen, Daniel. *Sarcosuchus Imperator*. Mankato, MN: Bridgestone Books (2003).

Markle, Sandra. *Crocodiles*. Minneapolis, MN: Carolrhoda Books (2004).

Walker, Sally M. *SuperCroc Found*. Minneapolis, MN: Millbrook Press (2006).

Learn More Online

Visit these Web sites to learn more about Paul Sereno and SuperCroc:

www.paulsereno.org/

www.projectexploration.org

www.supercroc.org

Index

About the Authors

Paleontologist **Paul Sereno** grew up in a suburb of Chicago, studied art and biology as an undergraduate, trained as a paleontologist in New York, and now is a professor at the University of Chicago and cofounder of Project Exploration. Discoverer of dinosaurs on five continents and leader of dozens of expeditions, Paul began his fieldwork in Argentina, where his team discovered the early dinosaur *Eoraptor*, and continued in the Sahara, where his teams unearthed dozens of dinosaurs and crocodilians, including the 40-foot-long (12-m) SuperCroc.

Natalie Lunis has written more than two dozen science and nature books for children. She hunts for fossils at the American Museum of Natural History in New York City.

About Project Exploration

Project Exploration is a nonprofit science education organization that was founded by paleontologist Paul Sereno and educator Gabrielle Lyon to make the wonders of science accessible—especially to minority youth and girls. For more information, visit **www.projectexploration.org**.